The
INSTRUMENTS
of MUSIC

The INSTRUMENTS of MUSIC

Guy L. Luttrell

publishers since 1798

THOMAS NELSON INC., PUBLISHERS

NASHVILLE   79-220   NEW YORK

Second printing

Library of Congress Cataloging in Publication Data
Luttrell, Guy L
    The instruments of music.

    Includes index.
    SUMMARY: Describes the human voice, instruments of the orchestra, American folk instruments, and the creation of musical sounds with electricity.
    1. Musical instruments—Juvenile literature.
[1. Musical instruments] I. Title.
ML3930.A2L85   781.9'1   77-11968
ISBN 0-8407-6559-2

Acknowledgments

I wish to thank the following for their assistance in providing illustrations: Baldwin Piano & Organ Company, C. G. Conn, J. C. Deagan, Inc., Fox Products Corp., Getzen Company Inc., G. Leblanc Corp., Ludwig Industries, The C. F. Martin Organisation, Norlin Music, Inc., Steinway & Sons, W and W Company, and the Shrine to Music, University of South Dakota.

In addition, portions of the chapters on brass, percussion, and electronic instruments are drawn from articles appearing in *Highlights for Children*, and are used with the permission of that magazine.

Contents

The
INSTRUMENTS
of MUSIC

1

About This Book

How does a harp player know which strings to pluck? Is the metal saxophone a brass or woodwind instrument? How does a clarinet reed work? Who invented the violin? What is the difference between the cornet and trumpet? These are excellent questions that are often asked of musicians. You will find the answers in this book.

Boys and girls always have a lot of good questions to ask about musical instruments. They enjoy the sounds the instruments make—some even play themselves—but they also want to know who, what, when, where, why, and how. For instance, whenever I demonstrate the French horn for students, they never fail to ask: "Why do you hold your hand inside the bell?" Jokingly, I tell them that I hold it there so that I can catch the wrong notes before they come out. Of course, that isn't the real reason, but the question is a good one and the answer is in the chapter on the history of horns.

Man has developed thousands of different kinds of musical instruments over the years. Each chapter in this book tells the story of a group or family of those instruments. Although many are no longer in existence, they were the ancestors of the instruments played in school bands today and heard making music every day on radio and television. In the following pages, you will read about more than fifty of today's most popular instruments as well as many of their ancestors. You will read how many of the instruments are made and played, and how to recognize them by their sights and sounds. You will even find suggestions on how to make your own instruments and create your own musical sounds.

Whether or not you can sing, read music, or play an instrument yourself, learning about the instruments of music will make the musical sounds you hear every day more interesting and exciting.

2

A Very Special Instrument

THE HUMAN VOICE—HOW IT WORKS, HOW IT IS USED

Man's oldest means of musical expression is the human voice. Many people consider it the most beautiful and sensitive of all musical instruments. This instrument is so personal that it is with you wherever you go, lets you make music whenever you want, can be used to make music without taking music lessons, and identifies you even when you can't be seen.

Just as no two people look exactly alike, no two voices sound exactly the same. Famous people are often recognized by their voices as well as their faces. In fact, we see entertainers on television who specialize in imitating the voices of famous people, but even though we might think that Rich Little, Frank Gorshin, and George Kirby sound just like actor John Wayne, they probably couldn't fool a close friend of his. Try calling one of your best friends on the telephone and don't identify yourself. It won't take long for him to recognize you by the sound of your voice. Although we all use the same kind of instrument to produce vocal sounds, the instrument is a part of our body and is very special.

The voice itself has changed very little since the earliest man used his to give a grunt or a snort, but its uses have changed a great deal. From the time of the very first grunt hundreds of thousands of years ago, man has experimented with the sounds he can make with his voice. He has learned that it can be used to scare away animals, imitate the sounds of nature, communicate with other people, and, most importantly for us, make music.

The human voice is a highly versatile instrument. Over the years, names have been given to the different kinds of sounds the voice can make: talking, cheering, shouting, whispering, crying, growling, mumbling, murmuring, hissing, calling, thundering, roaring, yelling. When the voice is used to make musical sounds, we call it singing.

Producing a sound with this instrument is simple—in fact, one of the first things a newborn baby does is cry—but how does it work? The first thing we do when we want to make a vocal sound is breathe air into our lungs. The air then starts its way back out by traveling up the trachea (windpipe) and through the larynx (voice box). Two tiny vocal cords inside the larynx begin vibrating as the air passes through and produce a very soft sound. This sound is then amplified by various resonators, including

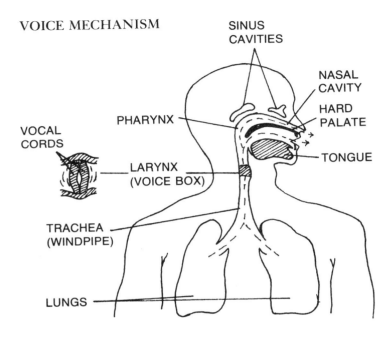

VOICE MECHANISM

SINUS CAVITIES

NASAL CAVITY

HARD PALATE

TONGUE

PHARYNX

VOCAL CORDS

LARYNX (VOICE BOX)

TRACHEA (WINDPIPE)

LUNGS

the pharynx, the sinus cavities, the nasal cavity, and the hard palate.

The sound that finally comes out of your mouth (and nose) depends on the position of your lips and tongue. To see how this works, take a breath and sing (or say) *ah*. As you sing the *ah*, raise and lower your tongue, and the sound will change from *ah* to *a* and then to an *ee* sound. While still singing an *ah*, slowly close your lips into a small circle and the sound will change from the *ah* to an *o* sound and then to *oo*.

Professional singers must know all of this. In addition they must practice their instruments many hours every day, doing breathing exercises, singing scales, and learning songs. Not many people want to become professional singers, but anyone can do some very simple things to improve his singing and make it more fun:

Sit or stand tall when you sing.

Always take a big breath before singing.

Each time you breathe, take the breath quickly through your mouth, as if you had just been scared by a ghost.

Don't move your shoulders or chest when breathing.

Sing easily. Singing too loud can hurt your voice.

Everyone can and should sing because it is fun, but to get the most pleasure from your voice, you must sing correctly. If you sing in a choir at school or in church, you have probably already learned that it is helpful to practice your singing just as you would practice any other instrument of music. Students who have learned to sing correctly learn to play other instruments more quickly and easily than nonsingers.

When singing just for the fun of it, most people will sing the same thing—the melody—and without music. When getting together to sing in an organized group, singers usually use written music and divide into parts, depending upon each singer's voice range. Women and girls with the highest voices will sing soprano, women and girls with lower voices sing alto, men with higher voices sing tenor, and men with the lowest voices will sing the bass part. A boy whose voice has not yet changed might sing either soprano, alto, or tenor, depending upon his voice range. (Oddly enough, boy sopranos often develop into basses as adults, and boy tenors often remain tenors as adults.) Each part has its own music to sing, and the parts fit together like a beautiful musical jigsaw puzzle.

Maybe you think that you can't sing because someone has said that you were a monotone or that you sing off-key. Don't you believe it. A monotone is a singer who sings everything on one note, because he has trouble distinguishing between high and low pitches. It doesn't mean that he *can't* sing different pitches—it only means that he hasn't yet learned how to do it. If you were a real monotone, you would probably talk on the same pitch, too. Try talking for five minutes without letting your voice go higher or lower; it will naturally try to go up and down. Your voice will do the same thing when you sing, but you must listen very carefully so that it goes higher or lower the right distance and at the right time.

If you are a boy whose voice is changing, perhaps you think you sound funny when your voice cracks or skips higher and lower. Don't let this stop you from singing. Your voice is part of your body and, just like your arms and legs, is growing from boy size to man size. All men have gone through this changing-voice period, and many have become famous singers.

People often sing when they are alone just to keep themselves company. When groups of people get together, it is natural that they sing. Sometimes they sing special songs such as "Happy Birthday" or the national anthem; sometimes they sing folk songs while gathered around a campfire in the woods or on a hayride; and at other times, they join together especially to sing and practice singing in choirs, glee clubs, or choruses.

The best thing about singing is that anyone can do it and have fun. Some people can sing better than others, but just as a young athlete doesn't have to be the fastest runner to enjoy running, so you don't have to be the best singer to enjoy singing. The fun of singing makes the voice one of the most popular instruments of music.

3

American Folk Instruments

THE GUITAR, FIDDLE, BANJO, AND MANY MORE

F olk music is music of the common people. Created by someone who has a story to tell rather than composed by a trained musician, it is simple and easy to understand. Folk songs have easy, singable melodies, use simple harmonies, and (unless the song tells a sad story) have rhythms that are fun for dancing. Many of America's folk songs tell the stories of cowboys, slaves, and railroad workers, people who led exciting and adventurous lives and enjoyed describing them in song.

The instruments of folk music are the instruments people happened to have around at the time. Many of those we associate with American folk music were brought to this country by the early settlers. Others were introduced in America by later immigrants from Europe, or by sailors, slaves, or inventive people who built their own instruments if no others were available.

The guitar and fiddle were probably the earliest instruments to find their way to America in the baggage of settlers. Both of these instruments have long histories and lead double lives. Their ancestors are the lutes, viols, rebecs, and other string instruments of past centuries. The guitar and fiddle play serious music in concert halls, and they accompany folk music and dancing in dance halls. In fact, the fiddle is really the name given to a violin when it is played in a popular or folk style.

Although a fiddle player at a country hoedown may not hold his instrument and bow exactly the same way as a violinist in a symphony orchestra does, they will both be using the same kind of instrument and playing it in much the same manner. The fiddle, like the violin, can only be played one or two notes at a time and usually plays the melody. Its customary place is in a group where other instruments play the harmonies and emphasize the rhythms. For bluegrass, country and western, and square-dance styles of music, the fiddle is usually joined by one or more guitars, a banjo, a drum set, and its oversized relative, the string bass.

The guitar was first brought to America by British and Spanish immigrants. It traveled with the settlers and became established as a basic folk instrument in all parts of our country. Carried by the lone cowboy watching his herd at night, played by people living in log cabins far from civilization, and joining the fiddle to provide music for barn dancing in frontier towns, the guitar became an American favorite.

SIX-
STRING
GUITAR

**TWELVE-
STRING
GUITAR**

X Still one of the most popular instruments of music, the guitar comes in many shapes and sizes. There are folk guitars, classical guitars, and electric guitars; there are guitars with four, six, and twelve strings; and there are guitars with the usual single neck as well as others with two necks. Although each guitar has been designed to play a certain type of music, all are played much the same and can be used for folk music.

Just like all of the instruments in folk music, the guitar can be played by anyone with an ear for music. You might learn to play it faster with the help of a teacher, but you can probably learn enough to accompany a folk song by experimenting and practicing on your own.

The guitar is either held on the player's lap or by a strap over the shoulder. The sound is produced by plucking and strumming the strings with either the fingers of the right hand or a plastic pick held between the thumb and forefinger. Different pitches are played by pressing, or stopping, the strings against the fingerboard with the fingers on the left hand.

The guitar fingerboard has metal strips (frets) across its face at regular intervals. These frets make it easier for the player to stop the strings at the right places. To play a melody, one string is played at a time. To play chords, several of the strings are strummed with the right hand and fingered with the left hand. By learning the left-hand fingerings for three or four chords and strumming the strings in rhythm, a player is ready to play the accompaniment of many different folk songs.

**ELECTRIC
GUITAR**

The banjo is played much like the guitar. The first banjos in America are believed to have been made by black slaves. The early instruments were much like open-backed skin-belly lutes still found in Africa. Their bodies were a round shell with a skin stretched across one side. A long, slender neck was attached to the body, and four strings were stretched the length of the neck. Modern banjos are much fancier, and they usually have five strings. The banjo holds an important place in the folk music of America.

Other stringed instruments used in folk music include the mandolin, ukulele, dulcimer, Autoharp, and zither. The mandolin is a pear-shaped instrument closely related to the lutes of early England. It has eight strings and is best known for its playing of the tremolo, a rapid down-and-up picking of the strings that creates a tremulous quaver.

The ukulele looks like a very small guitar with four strings. It is usually associated with hula dancers and the Hawaiian Islands. (The name is Hawaiian and means "jumping flea.") However, its small size made it a popular instrument in the United States long before Hawaii became a state. In the early 1900's many popular singers used the ukulele to accompany themselves as they sang. People throughout the country found that the uke was easily carried wherever they might go as well as easy and fun to play. The uke isn't as popular today as it was then, but it is still an important instrument in much folk music.

The dulcimer and Autoharp are also easy and fun to play, but like the uke are played by relatively few people.

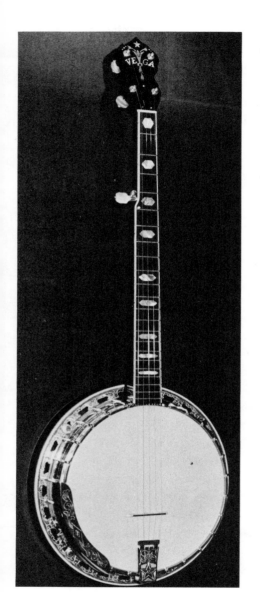

MANDOLIN

FIVE-STRING BANJO

The Appalachian or mountain dulcimer is similar to folk instruments found in the Scandinavian countries. It is held on the lap, and the melody string is plucked with one finger. Different pitches are made by stopping the string with a small stick held in the left hand. Its soft, clear tones are just right to accompany lullabies and songs telling sad stories.

The Autoharp was first made in Germany during the 1800's. It has many strings that provide sweeping, harplike chords when strummed. The instrument has a series of buttons to be pressed while playing. Each button is attached to dampers which cut out certain strings. The buttons usually have the name of a chord written on top, and the player merely has to press down the button for the chord he wants to play and strum the strings with either a finger or a felt pick. The Autoharp is an easy folk instrument and fun to play, and in addition it has become widely used for teaching music in schools.

A similar, but more complicated instrument is the zither. This is a folk instrument from northern Europe that has thirty to forty strings stretched across a flat, hollow sound box. The top four strings are used for playing the melody, while the rest of the strings are plucked and strummed to provide the accompaniment. The right hand plucks and strums, and the left hand stops the melody strings against the frets of a guitarlike fingerboard. When Johann Strauss composed his famous waltz "Tales from the Vienna Woods," he included a charming solo for the zither in the orchestral score.

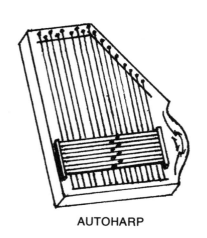

AUTOHARP

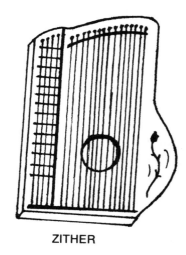

ZITHER

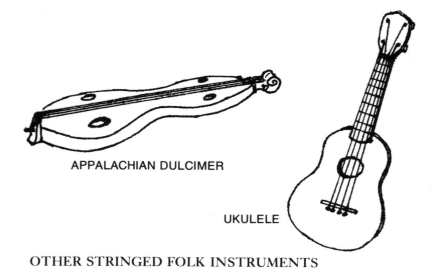

APPALACHIAN DULCIMER

UKULELE

OTHER STRINGED FOLK INSTRUMENTS

The concertina and accordion are both combination wind-and-reed instruments. Each has a bellows that produces a flow of air as it is pumped in and out by the player's arms. This air flow passes across a series of reeds, housed in cases at each end of the bellows, which vibrate to make the sound. The reeds are operated by buttons or keys, which the player presses with the fingers of both hands. Because of the pumping action of the bellows, which are held in front of the player, these instruments have been given the popular nicknames of "squeeze box" and "belly pincher."

The concertina was a favorite instrument of men working on the sailing ships of the 1800's. It was both easy to play and small enough to be easily stowed away during a voyage. It probably sailed across the ocean to America with the early settlers to join the guitar and fiddle in accompanying folk music and dancing.

The concertina was played by pressing buttons with both hands, but, in the 1850's, a keyboard replaced the right-hand buttons, and the modern accordion was born. The accordion is much larger than the concertina and more complex. Each key of the right-hand fingerboard produces one note. The buttons played with the left hand produce either a bass note or a chord. Because of its complexity, which requires the player to press keys and buttons with both hands while he pumps the bellows, the accordion requires considerable practice. Although the concertina remains an important instrument in much folk

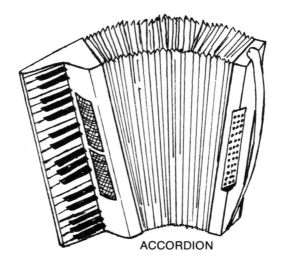

ACCORDION

HARMONICA

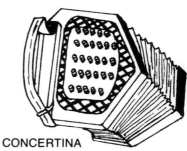

CONCERTINA

WIND-REED FOLK INSTRUMENTS

music, the accordion has become more important in the fields of jazz and popular music.

The harmonica might be called a pocket accordion. It is small enough to be held in one hand, and its small case contains a series of reeds like those used in the accordion and concertina. By blowing through small openings in the case, the reeds are made to vibrate and produce the harmonica's sound. The idea of blowing air across a thin reed that is free to vibrate was used in instruments made of bamboo over three thousand years ago in the Orient. However, the harmonica as we know it wasn't developed until 1829. It is one of the youngest of all folk instruments.

The tone quality of the harmonica is similar to that of the accordion and concertina, only much softer. It is also called a mouth organ because its reed tone is similar to some of the tones played on a pipe organ. Since it can stand a lot of rough handling without going badly out of tune and is so small, the harmonica has become a favorite of people who travel with very little baggage, such as soldiers, sailors, and those who do a lot of hiking and camping.

The remaining folk instruments are more sound makers than musical instruments. The kazoo, for example, doesn't really produce a musical sound but alters the sound of the player's voice as he hums into the mouth hole. A similar sound can be made by folding a piece of tissue paper over a comb and humming through the paper. The Jews' harp is another sound maker and one of the oldest known. It consists of a small metal frame around a thin metal tongue. The frame is held in front of the player's open mouth as he plucks the metal tongue with his fingers. The twanging sound of the vibrating tongue is then amplified by the player's mouth.

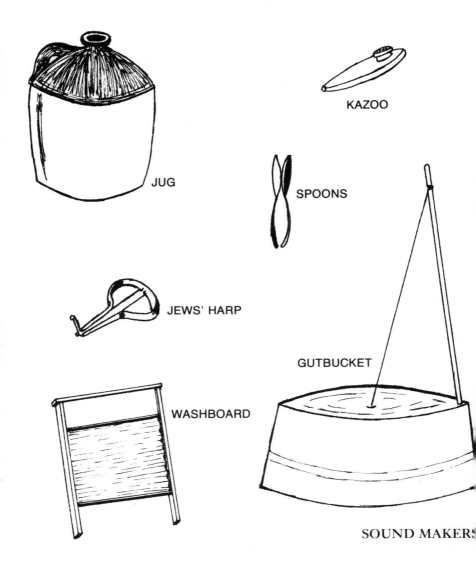

JUG

KAZOO

SPOONS

JEWS' HARP

GUTBUCKET

WASHBOARD

SOUND MAKERS

Other sound-making instruments are the jug, gutbucket, washboard, and spoons. Blowing across the top of a big jug produces a deep-sounding *hoomph* that is used to provide rhythms. The gutbucket (washtub bass) is an upside-down washtub with a pole stood on top. A rope, or string, is stretched from a hole in the middle of the tub to the top of the pole. The string is held tight and plucked like a string bass. The sound is a deep *thump* that can be made higher or lower by tightening and loosening the string.

The washboard is played by strumming its ridges with thimbles on the player's fingers. In playing the spoons, a pair of them are held between the fingers so that the bowls of the spoons will clack together. Both the washboard and spoons are used to provide rhythm in some folk music. Like the other sound makers, there is no right or wrong way to play them. They are inexpensive to buy (or easy to make) and fun to play.

The most popular of all folk instruments, of course, cost nothing, and everyone has them. There is no better instrument than the voice for singing and telling the story. For providing rhythms, no instrument is more capable than the clapping of hands and stamping of feet. Anytime there is a hootenanny (a gathering of folk musicians), there will be guitar players, fiddlers, banjo pickers, and gutbucket players, but everyone will join in by singing, clapping, and stamping.

4

The Heart of the Orchestra

THE VIOLIN FAMILY—VIOLIN, VIOLA, CELLO, DOUBLE BASS

S tarting with a design that is nearly four hundred years old, the violin maker selects just the right pieces of wood from his storeroom. Each part of the instrument will be made from a special kind of wood, and he chooses pieces of spruce, maple, pine, ebony, or Pernambuco wood with which to work.

For the next three or four months the instrument maker will carve, shape, and fit these pieces of wood together like a puzzle. As he finishes each of the nearly seventy different parts, it will be fitted in the proper place. Some parts will be glued, others will be held in the proper position by being fitted just right, but no nails or screws are used. With all of the parts in place, the instrument will be given several coats of varnish. Finally, when the last coat of varnish is dry, four steel or gut strings will be stretched tightly across the instrument's hollow body, and a new member of the violin family is ready to be played.

The player makes the strings vibrate to produce the sound by either plucking (pizzicato) or drawing a bow across them (arco). Although the sound of a vibrating string is very soft, the instrument's body vibrates along, or in sympathy, with the string. This sympathetic vibration, especially of the large surfaces of the belly and back, adds resonance and volume to the tone.

The string's vibrations are first transmitted through the bridge to the belly. They are then spread over a wide area by the bass bar and carried to the back through the sound post. The amplified tone then travels out the sound holes to the listener. Depending upon the instrument's size, the tone will either be the beautiful, singing sound of a violin, the warm, dark sound of a viola, the rich sound of a cello, or the gruff sound of a double bass.

The history of the violin family goes back several thousand years, but the violin's most important ancestors are found during the ninth to sixteenth centuries. Musicians in Germany were making music on the lira and fidicula during this time. In the Orient they played the tube zither, and troubadours accompanied their singing on the vielle and viol in many parts of Europe. During the sixteenth century, the musicians of India played instruments called the sarangi and sarinda, in Greece they played the lyre, and in Arabia the rebec.

All of these instruments used a vibrating string to make their sound and were played either pizzicato or arco.

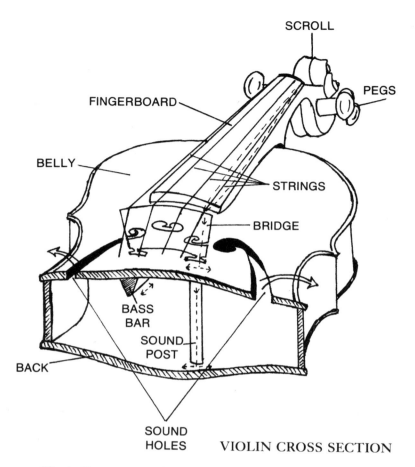

SCROLL

PEGS

FINGERBOARD

BELLY

STRINGS

BRIDGE

BASS
BAR

SOUND
POST

BACK

SOUND
HOLES   VIOLIN CROSS SECTION

The bridge supports the strings and transmits their vibrations to the belly (top). The bass bar is a narrow strip of wood about ten inches long glued to the underside of the belly. It helps distribute the vibrations over a wide area. The sound post is a cylindrical piece of wood about a quarter inch in diameter. It is fitted securely between the belly and back and carries the vibrations to the back. The bass bar and sound post also help strengthen the instrument's hollow body. The amplified tone comes out the sound holes. Note the absence of frets from the neck, or fingerboard.

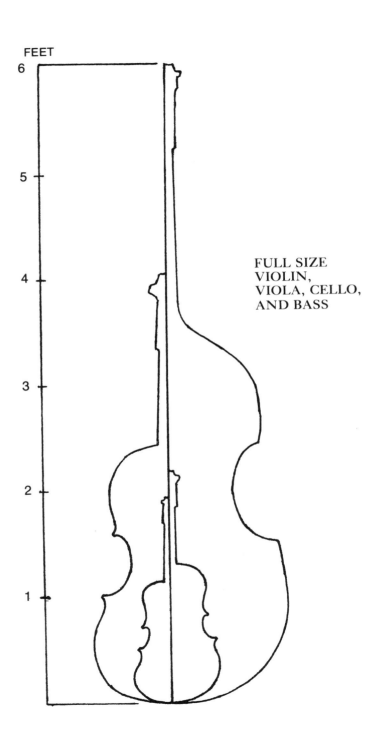

FEET

FULL SIZE
VIOLIN,
VIOLA, CELLO,
AND BASS

Although their names are unfamiliar to us today, they led to the development of the first violin by Gasparo da Salò, an instrument maker of northern Italy, in the late 1500's. With the development of the viola, cello, and double bass, the violin family was complete, and it quickly became an important group of instruments throughout Europe.

From the time of the first violin until about 1750, the most famous makers lived in the little Italian town of Cremona. During that period, members of the Amati and Guarneri families made such beautiful instruments that they are still played and prized by professional musicians.

The master of all of the Cremona violin makers was a student of Amati—Antonio Stradivari. His instruments also are still played by some of today's greatest musicians. There are many fine violin makers in the world, but none has been able to discover exactly what causes a Strad to produce such a beautiful tone. About six hundred of the eleven hundred instruments made by Stradivari during his lifetime are still in existence, and each is valued at tens of thousands of dollars. The finest of today's string instruments are still made like those of Amati, Guarneri, and Stradivari. Even those used by beginning students are of the same design developed by the masters of Cremona.

The bow used in playing the instruments of the violin family is largely responsible for the richness of tone, variety of expression, and singing quality that characterizes them. Originating among the nomads of Central Asia in the eighth century, the bow didn't take on its present shape until nearly a thousand years later. The man responsible for developing the modern bow was a Frenchman named François Tourte, often called the Stradivari of the bow because of his important contribution to string playing.

The early bows consisted of a curved stick with horsehair stretched tightly between the ends of the stick,

EVOLUTION OF THE BOW

HUNTER'S BOW

SEVENTEENTH-CENTURY VIOLIN BOW

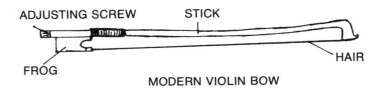

ADJUSTING SCREW   STICK

HAIR

FROG

MODERN VIOLIN BOW

much like a hunter's bow. This kind of bow was not only awkward to handle but difficult to adjust. The design of later bows improved both of these areas by curving the stick inward toward the hair for better balance and fastening one end of the hair to a device called a frog, which makes it easy for the player to adjust the tension of the hair by turning a small knob. In the 1700's, Tourte took this design and refined it to make what many players still consider to be the perfect bow.

A modern bow stick is fifteen to twenty inches long, made from Pernambuco wood, and weighs only a few ounces. Although it is very simple in design, a professional player knows how important a bow is to his playing and will pay several hundred dollars for a fine Tourte bow.

Attending a symphony orchestra concert for the first time, you might be surprised to see that two thirds of the one hundred musicians are playing instruments of the violin family. To the left of the conductor are thirty-six musicians playing violins. The violin section is divided into two groups—first violins and second violins. There is no difference in the instruments that are used in each group, only in the parts that they play. Just like the soprano singers in a choir, the first violins usually play the highest part and the melody; the second violins play an alto part, which is lower in pitch.

The violinists hold their instruments between the jaw and shoulder while drawing the bow across the strings. If the bow is drawn smoothly, the sound is smooth or legato.

VIOLIN

Sometimes the bow is bounced on the strings (spiccato) and at other times it is moved back and forth rapidly (tremolo). Each use of the bow makes a different kind of sound, and every player in the section must use his bow in exactly the same manner.

In addition to the tones of the four "open" strings, the players make many other tones by stopping the string with the fingers of their left hands. When a string is pressed against the fingerboard, its length is shortened, and a higher sound is produced. The closer to the sound box the finger is pressed, the higher the note. There is nothing on the fingerboard to tell a player exactly where to place his fingers (that is, unlike a guitar, a violin has no frets), he must listen very carefully and practice hard to learn where the right spots are for each note.

Sometimes the player will draw the bow across two strings at a time, and this is called a double stop. By using double stops, a skillful player can play two melodies at one time, making it sound as though two violins were playing a duet.

Just in front and to the right of the conductor is another section of twelve to fourteen musicians playing instruments that look much like the violins. This is the viola section. Violas are played, held, and look like violins; however, they are about two inches longer than violins, have larger bodies and a deeper tone. Violas are the tenor voice of the string family and play either melody, countermelody, or in combination with other instruments.

Directly to the right of the conductor is the cello sec-

VIOLA

tion. Even though the cellos are shaped like violins and violas, there is no chance of confusing them. The cellos are not only much larger than the others but have lower sounds. The player sits on a chair and holds the body of the cello between his knees as he plays. Although it is held much differently from the violin, the cello is played much the same; the strings are either plucked or bowed, and different pitches are made by stopping the strings with the fingers of the left hand.

As with players in the other sections, the ten to twelve cellists practice many hours so that they can play perfectly together. Cellos often play bass parts, but when they play a melody, it seems to sing out in a strong, rich baritone voice. So beautiful is their tone that Camille Saint-Saëns uses the cello to describe the majestic movement of the swan in *Carnival of the Animals*.

Behind the cello section are the double basses. They are also called string basses or bass viols (or fiddles)—and sometimes, just for fun, dog houses. They are so big that the player either sits on a high stool or stands next to the instrument, so low that even the tuba can't match their sound, and so powerful that there are only six to nine of them in a large orchestra. When the double bass is plucked, the strings make a deep, resonant sound that helps keep the rhythm. This makes it a popular instrument in jazz and popular music. When it is played arco, it sounds very low and grumbly and is sometimes called upon to play either mysterious or unusual melodies. In *Carnival of the Animals*, the double basses play the theme of the lumbering elephants.

CELLO

Each instrument of the violin family is made in many different sizes. There are eighteen different sizes of violins, violas, cellos, and double basses—an instrument to fit any size of player. A five-year-old boy or girl can begin study on a small-size violin and, as he or she grows, transfer to gradually larger instruments until he is big enough to play a full-sized violin.

The instruments of the violin family are equally at home playing solos, in small groups, or in large orchestras. One of the most popular small ensembles is the string quartet—two violins, one viola, and one cello. Each instrument in the string quartet is equally important, sometimes playing melody, sometimes playing accompaniment. The *Emperor Quartet*, one of over eighty string quartets composed by Joseph Haydn, is in the form of a theme and variations and gives each instrument a chance to play the melody. A string quintet is a string quartet with a part of equal importance added for the double bass.

Composers often write music for the string orchestra, which is like a string quintet with many players playing each part. When Mozart composed *Eine Kleine Nachtmusik*, it was written to be played by a string quintet. However, it is usually performed by a string orchestra and is, perhaps, even lovelier with several musicians playing each of the five parts.

A symphony orchestra is made up of the strings plus sections of brass, woodwind, and percussion instruments. In *Young Person's Guide to the Orchestra*, Benjamin Britten illustrates the sounds of these various sections and how

BASS VIOL

they are joined together. Certainly, there is no sound as exciting as that of a symphony orchestra with its variety of woodwind sounds, blaring brasses, and crashing cymbals, especially when they are playing music by Tchaikovsky, Richard Strauss, and the other great composers. Nevertheless, the strings remain the most important section. Their beautiful tones, versatility, and general usefulness have earned the instruments of the violin family the title "heart of the orchestra."

5

A History of Horns

THE BRASS FAMILY—TRUMPET, FRENCH HORN, TROMBONE, TUBA, SOUSAPHONE, CORNET, BARITONE HORN

Thousands of years ago man discovered that by boring a hole in the side of an animal horn and forcing air through the opening, he could produce sounds that were useful in sending messages short distances. The sound was generated by the player's either buzzing his lips into the small opening or by blowing across the opening as you would blow across the top of a Coke bottle. The horn then amplified the sound and made it loud enough to be heard some distance away.

Since buzzing the lips into the opening produced the louder sound, this was probably the method most used by early man, and it is the method used today in producing the sound on instruments we call horns. It's easy to produce a sound by buzzing your lips: lick your lips, close them by saying the letter *m*, tighten the muscles at the corners of your mouth, and force air between your lips. Professional musicians can actually play songs by tightening and relaxing their lips as they buzz. Although the discovery of how to make a sound using an animal horn probably excited early man, he soon began trying to improve the instrument he was using. To produce a sound loud enough to travel many miles, he needed a very large horn, larger than most animal horns, so he made instruments out of wood in the shape of animal horns. People living in the Alps of Switzerland play wooden Alpine horns twelve feet long. Many years ago, these giant instruments were used to send messages from mountain to mountain.

As metals and their uses became known to man, people began to make horns out of them. Metal horns could be made different lengths, sizes, and shapes to produce different sounds. A metal tube two feet long would produce a very high sound, a tube eight feet long would produce a low sound, a cone-shaped tube produced a mellow sound, and a tube with straight sides, like a piece of pipe, would produce a shrill sound.

As horns and horn playing developed, it was found that different tones could be played on one horn. One method was for the player to tighten and relax his lips as he buzzed into the horn. The other method was to bore holes in the horn, which could be left open or covered with a finger. Both methods helped the player produce different tones that allowed him to play very simple melodies as well as send messages.

The horn player was now buzzing his lips into a small cup-shaped mouthpiece at the end of his horn. This change, along with the invention of a valve mechanism in 1815, which opened and closed holes leading to extra pieces of tubing attached to the horn, allowed the player to play every note in the chromatic scale. Horns could now

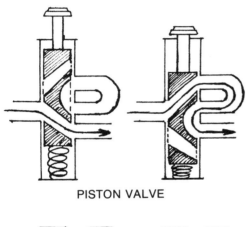

PISTON VALVE

Piston valves are used on most brass instruments, but the French horn and some tubas use the rotary valve. When a valve is open, the sound passes straight through, but when a valve is closed, the sound must detour through an added piece of tubing. Since it travels farther, the tone is lower—the longer the detour, the lower the tone.

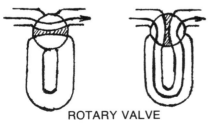

ROTARY VALVE

VALVE MECHANISMS

make real music, and they would soon be an important family in the orchestra, playing complicated melodies and beautiful harmonies.

One of the biggest problems faced by horn makers was how to make a horn long enough to sound in the right range while still being compact enough for the player to hold easily. The solution was to bend the tube in some way. However, since bending the tube also changed the sound a little, horn makers tried many different shapes before finding the best shape for each instrument.

The involute trumpet, an instrument from the year 1598, looked like a pretzel; the brass serpent from the early 1600's had so many twists and turns that it resembled a big snake, hence its name; and some of the early hunting horns had their tubing coiled very tightly in a circle, much as you might coil a garden hose.

Although there are many different horns in the modern brass family, the most important ones are the trumpet, French horn, trombone, and tuba. Each instrument plays in a different range, is shaped differently, and has certain types of music that it plays best.

The exciting sound of the trumpet and its ancestors has impressed people throughout history. It is the smallest and highest-sounding brass instrument and is often heard playing fanfares at important occasions. In the Middle Ages, the noblemen of England and Europe each had his own trumpet call. Monarchs, including Henry VIII of England, even maintained special bands of trumpeters to play their special calls at royal ceremonies and pageants.

TRUMPET

Of course, the early trumpets were much like their cousin, the bugle. They were similar in shape, neither one had valves, and they were capable of producing only a few different tones, the number depending upon the player's skill in buzzing his lip. Over the years, the bugle has remained much the same, an instrument of few notes whose chief use is communicating military messages across long distances. One of the best-known bugle calls is still heard at football games. Once used to signal soldiers to charge the enemy, today it is used to signal football players that their fans want them to "charge" to the touchdown. Other widely known bugle calls are taps and the race-track call.

Meanwhile, the trumpet developed into the leading instrument of the brass family. Instrument makers experimented to find the best metals to use in making trumpets and added valves; composers began writing special music for the trumpet, and included it as an important instrument in the orchestra; and trumpet players learned to play not only bugle calls but all kinds of music.

Even though the tone of the trumpet is very brilliant, it is capable of playing beautiful melodies. When its sound is blended with that of other instruments, new and exciting sounds are created. As with all brass instruments, the tone of the trumpet can be altered by placing a mute in the bell.

TRUMPET MUTES

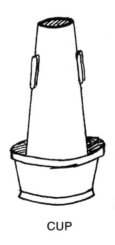

STRAIGHT   CUP

This is a cone-shaped device usually made of metal or fiberboard. A muted trumpet has a soft, faraway sound and is often used to represent an echo of the sounds of other instruments.

At one time in its history, only men were allowed to play the trumpet. Today, both men and women play the trumpet, and thousands of boys and girls play it in school orchestras and bands. The trumpet's exciting sounds are heard wherever music is played.

The hunting horn, ancestor of the French horn, was usually coiled in a circle so that the player could carry it over his shoulder while "riding to the hounds" on horseback. Although the French horn is no longer carried in this manner, it is still coiled in much the same way. If it were stretched out straight, the French horn would be approximately twelve to sixteen feet long and shaped like a cone, being very small at the end the player buzzes into and very large at the bell end.

The player rests the large end of the French horn on his right leg while playing and holds his hand partway inside of the bell. Before the invention of valves, the player would adjust his hand inside the bell to produce different notes. This can still be done, but since the valve has made it possible for the player to produce every note of the chromatic scale, the right hand is only used as a type of mute.

When the player's hand is in its normal position partway inside the bell, it softens the tone of the French horn and makes it very mellow. Placed all the way inside the

FRENCH HORN

bell, the hand "stops" the sound and makes it very nasal and brassy. Sometimes the player is instructed to remove his hand from the bell altogether and hold the bell pointing upward. When played this way, the tone is louder and more brilliant, just right for imitating the shrieks of trumpeting elephants.

The French horn has many personalities. Tchaikovsky wrote a beautiful solo for the mellow sound of the French horn in his Symphony No. 5. It's one of the most famous melodies in music. The wide range of the instrument is called for in *Till Eulenspiegel's Merry Pranks* by Richard Strauss. Although the solo is rather short, the player must produce a rapid series of notes that go as high as a trumpet and as low as a tuba. And, of course, the French horn can be heard playing elephant "rips" and fanfares during exciting television shows.

The trombone has changed very little throughout its history and would have been as easy to spot three hundred years ago as it is today. Instead of having valves like other brasses, it has a U-shaped section of movable tubing that the player slides in and out to change pitches. This section of tubing is called a slide. By moving the slide out, the length of the trombone tubing is made longer and the pitch lower. As the slide is moved in, the tubing length is shortened, and the pitch gets higher. Just like the instruments of the violin family, there is nothing to tell the player where to put the slide for exactly the right note. The trombonist must practice hard and listen carefully to learn where these spots are.

When the slide is moved in and out without stopping, the trombone makes a comical sound called a glissando. Although beginners often make this sound by accident as they try to find the right note, a skillful player plays the

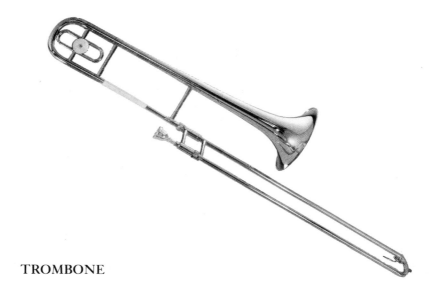

TROMBONE

glissando on purpose. It is most often heard in jazz and
dixieland music, but it is also employed as a special effect
in serious band and orchestra music. An example of this
may be heard in the finale of Maurice Ravel's "Bolero."

The tuba, largest and lowest-sounding of the brasses,
has eighteen feet of tubing coiled so that the player can
hold it on his lap as he plays. In order to make the tuba
easier for the players in a marching band to carry, the
sousaphone was developed in the early 1900's. Named for
bandmaster John Philip Sousa, the sousaphone is a tuba
coiled in a big circle. The player gets inside the circle and
rests the weight of the instrument on his shoulder as he
marches. A metal sousaphone might weigh as much as
fifty pounds, but many are now being made of fiberglass
and are much lighter.

The sound of the tuba is very low and grumbly. Played alone, it doesn't seem to have much power, but as the bass of the brass section, one tuba can balance the powerful sounds of several trumpets, French horns, and trombones. When just the brass section plays, it is called a brass choir, and the sound is very impressive.

In a symphony orchestra there are usually three trumpets, four French horns, three trombones, and one tuba. In a band, there are generally two or three times as many of these instruments as well as some others not used in the orchestra. The most common of these are the cornet and baritone horn.

The cornet is a cousin of the trumpet. It plays in the same range, looks much like the trumpet, and often com-

CORNET

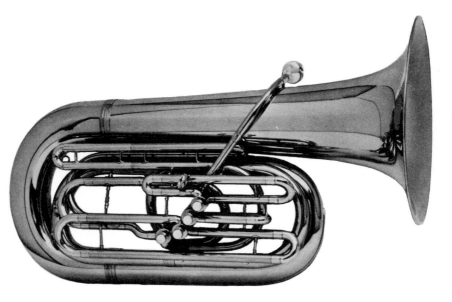

TUBA

FIBERGLASS SOUSAPHONE

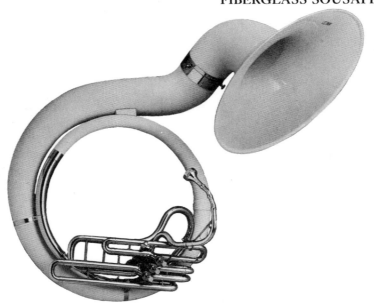

pletely replaces the trumpet as the soprano of the brass section in a band. The chief differences are that the cornet is coiled a little differently, and the tubing is more like a cone. These differences make the cornet shorter and easier to handle, and less brilliant sounding than the trumpet.

The baritone horn looks like a small tuba. It is half as big as the tuba and plays in the same range as the trombone. The sound of the baritone is more mellow than the trombone, and because it uses valves rather than a slide, plays its own separate part. The baritone is sometimes called the cello of the band because of its mellow tone.

BARITONE HORN

Whether you are listening to a marching band, a symphony orchestra, or the background music on a television show, the horns of the brass family provide some of the most exciting sounds you will hear.

6

The Wide World of Woodwinds

FLUTE, CLARINET, SAXOPHONE, AND DOUBLE REED

The earliest woodwind instrument known to man dates back to the pipes of Pan. Pan was the Greek god of the forest, flocks, and shepherds in Green mythology. He is usually pictured as half man and half goat—head and torso of a man, legs and feet of a goat—and is shown playing a set of pipes.

Shepherds of that time no doubt played instruments like this to keep themselves company while watching over their flocks in the hills of ancient Greece. With one pipe they could play tones of different lengths in a monotonous one-note melody. By bundling several together, like the pipes of Pan, they could play simple tunes.

The pipes were several hollow reeds of different lengths tied together. Each reed had a small notch cut through its side near the top. When the piper blew through one of the

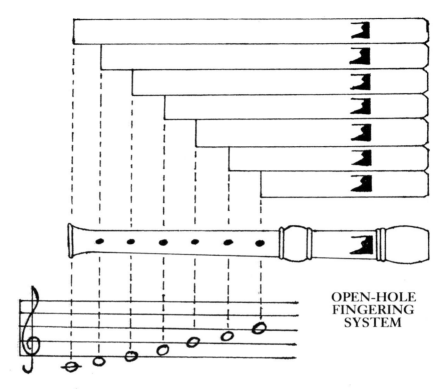

OPEN-HOLE
FINGERING
SYSTEM

reeds, the notch split the air column and caused the air inside to vibrate. In the longer pipes the vibrating air produced a low sound, and as the pipes got gradually shorter, the sound became higher.

As the pipes developed, someone discovered that one pipe could do the work of many if it had evenly spaced holes cut in the side. With all of the holes covered by fingers, the sound came out the end of the pipe, producing the first note of a scale. When the bottom finger was lifted, the sound came out of that hole, creating the second note of the scale. And by opening the remaining holes one at a time, the piper could play the other notes of the scale.

This open-hole system of playing different pitches was also used on two other kinds of early woodwinds—single reed and double reed. Both types of instruments probably originated in the Orient and used either one or two small pieces of reed cane to produce their sounds.

The sound of a single-reed woodwind is produced by blowing across a very thin piece of cane attached to a

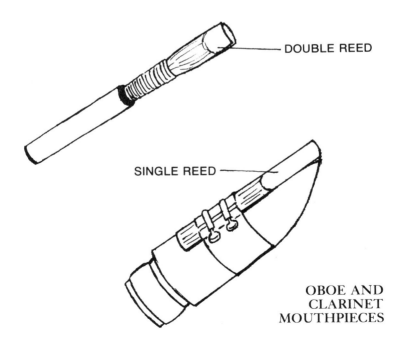

DOUBLE REED

SINGLE REED

OBOE AND
CLARINET
MOUTHPIECES

hollow tube. The air striking the reed sets it into rapid vibration. The hollow tube acts as an amplifier for the soft sound made by the reed. You can produce a single-reed sound with your thumbs and a blade of grass. With your thumbs side by side, hold the blade of grass so that it stretches tightly across the opening between them. If you blow through the opening just right, the blade of grass will vibrate and produce a squawking sound.

Double-reed woodwinds have two pieces of very thin cane attached to the pipe. As the player blows air through the pipe, both reeds vibrate and produce a very nasal sound. If you have a paper drinking straw, you can make a simple double-reed instrument. Pinch one end of the straw and cut the corners off evenly. Now, hold the flattened end of the straw lightly between your lips and blow gently. It might take several tries to produce a sound, but when you do, both sides of the straw will be vibrating just like a double-reed instrument.

The most important advance for woodwind instruments was the addition of keys to cover the holes used for making different pitches. Although on a woodwind with six finger holes one could play a major scale and all but one note of a chromatic scale by covering the holes in various combinations, many of the fingerings were awkward and the tones out of tune. The first key was added in the late 1600's so that the missing chromatic note could be played. Over the next two hundred years instrument makers experimented by boring additional holes and adding more keys to make fingering the woodwind instruments easier. Thus they became more versatile and playable.

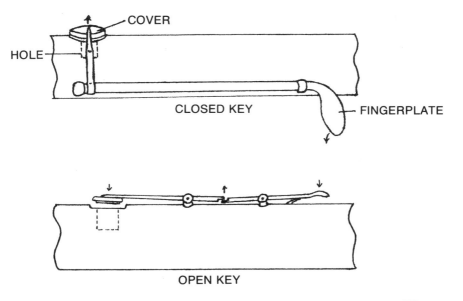

WOODWIND KEYS

These are the two main types of woodwind keys. The closed key covers a hole until the player presses the fingerplate. This action raises the cover and allows the tone to come out of that hole. The open key does just the opposite, remaining open until the player presses the fingerplate.

Although the key mechanism on modern woodwind instruments looks very complicated to a beginner, all the keys, rings, rods, and springs actually make the fingering much easier; ten fingers can now do the work of twenty. If a student practices hard, he will soon be playing much faster music than even a professional could play 250 years ago.

Since the time of the pipes of Pan in ancient Greece, hundreds of woodwind instruments have come and gone.

All of these instruments have had two things in common: they were played by blowing air through a hollow tube, and they had finger holes in the side to change pitch (either with or without keys). Over the past 150 years materials other than wood have been used to make woodwind instruments, but they are still played the same way and classified as woodwinds even when their bodies are made from plastic or metal.

The woodwind instruments of today are not grouped into one family but four families—flute, clarinet, saxophone, and double reed. The oldest is the flute family, and paintings of ancient Egypt and Greece show that flutelike instruments were highly prized by those early peoples.

Descendants of the pipes of Pan, flutes of those times were held vertically and had a mouthpiece like a whistle. The player would blow into the mouthpiece, and the notch near the end would start the air vibrating to produce the sound. They were much like the recorders and song flutes used in school music classes today.

Sometime during the Middle Ages, an unknown flute player found that the flute could be played by blowing directly across the notch, or blowhole, just as you blow across the top of a pop bottle. The notch had to be shaped a bit differently, and the flute held to the side, but the tone was very pleasing and could be controlled better by the player. From that time on, the flute as we know it gradually developed.

The tone of the modern flute is very pleasant to listen

to, and it usually plays the melody. The flute's tone is soft
and warm in the low part of its range, but in its higher
range the tone becomes more brilliant. Rapid passages are
often given to the flutes because of their remarkable agil-
ity. A favorite special effect of the flute is an imitation of
the chirping of birds, and Serge Prokofieff, in his *Peter and
the Wolf,* uses the flute to represent the bird in his story.

The flute is a soprano instrument of the woodwinds,

FLUTE

PICCOLO

and it can play a full octave (eight notes) higher than the soprano voice can sing. The piccolo might be called a double soprano, because it is just half as big as a flute and can play two full octaves higher than the soprano voice. The tone of the piccolo is shrill and piercing, capable of being heard above the sound of a large symphony orchestra playing its loudest. One of the piccolo's most famous solos is in John Philip Sousa's march "Stars and Stripes Forever."

Another small relative of the flute is the military fife. As early as the thirteenth century, the fife and side drum (snare drum) were used to accompany marching soldiers. However, unlike the piccolo, the fife has changed little over the years. It still uses the open hole system of fingering with, perhaps, one or two keys. Despite its limitations, the fife, along with the bugle and snare drum, has been important in military music for seven hundred years.

Other members of the flute family are the alto and bass flutes. These instruments aren't used often, but composers sometimes write music for them when they want the warm sound of the flute's low range with more power than the flute is capable of producing. The alto flute is several inches longer than the flute and plays four notes lower. The bass flute is even longer and can play a full octave lower than the flute. In fact, the bass flute is so long that the end with the blowhole is usually curved in a U so that it can be held more comfortably. The unusual tones of these larger flutes have made them popular jazz instruments.

BASS FLUTE

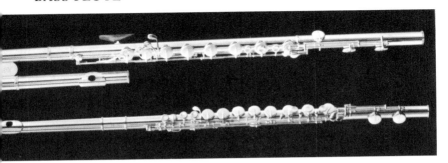

ALTO FLUTE

All the instruments of the flute family are very similar. Their sound is produced by a vibrating air column, they are all fingered the same way, and they are made from metal. The most important of the five is the flute, and when music is written for any of the others, it becomes the flutist's job to play them as well. Although it is a small family and the instruments can't play very loudly, the flute family has an important place in both our musical heritage and the music of today.

Instruments of the clarinet family are perhaps the most versatile and useful of the woodwinds. Descendants of a family of seventeenth-century instruments called shawms, shalmeys, or chalumeaux, their sounds are produced by blowing air across a single reed. The reed is fastened securely to a mouthpiece, a short hollow tube tapered at the end, with a metal band called a ligature. The tip of both the reed and mouthpiece are held in the

B-FLAT CLARINET

player's mouth, and when air is blown through the mouthpiece, the reed makes a squawking sound similar to the sound you made with the blade of grass. With the mouthpiece joined to the body of the clarinet, the sound is transformed into a rich, reedy tone.

As with the instruments of the violin family, clarinets come in many sizes, and each has its own special tone quality. The most common clarinet is the B-flat soprano. Beginning clarinet students nearly always start on this instrument. It is the one most frequently used in bands and orchestras (though clarinetists playing in orchestras often substitute the slightly smaller A clarinet for the B-flat soprano). There is a smaller clarinet, the E-flat soprano, which like the piccolo could be called a double soprano. It is several inches shorter than the B-flat soprano and can play very high notes. All three instruments have a beautiful singing-tone quality in their middle and upper ranges and usually play the melody. Their lower ranges are dark and reedy, perfect for playing background music when others have the melody.

There are four larger clarinets—alto, bass, contra-alto, and contrabass. Each can play four or five notes lower than the clarinet next smaller in size. The alto and bass have a rich, deep tone that sounds very mysterious. The contra-alto and contrabass can play the lowest, and their sound begins to sound grumbly in their lower range, almost like a soft rumbling in the distance rather than a musical tone.

Instruments of the clarinet family have three different shapes. The three smallest clarinets are hollow black tubes made from either ebonite (hard plastic) or grenadilla wood (a very hard wood that comes from the West Indies). The alto and bass clarinets have a similar black tube-shaped body but are longer and have a metal upturned bell at one end and a metal neck that the mouthpiece fits into at the other.

Instrument makers have tried making all of the clarinets with metal bodies, but only the contra-alto and contrabass are still made entirely of metal. Their bodies are long metal tubes (six to eight feet) doubled back and forth like a tight S. They are held in front of the player like all of the clarinets but have a supporting rod on the bottom that rests on the floor to help support the instrument's weight. With all of the necessary key mechanism attached to the body, these instruments are said to resemble a plumber's nightmare.

All of the clarinets are played the same way, and the music is written the same for them all. A clarinet player can "double" by playing several sizes of instrument; only a

CLARINET FAMILY

From left to right: E-flat Soprano, A Soprano, B-flat Soprano, Alto, Bass, Contrabass
Shrine to Music Museum, University of South Dakota

little practice is needed to get used to the differences in size and sound.

The newest family of woodwind instruments are the saxophones. These instruments have changed very little during their short history. A saxophone player of today could play the original saxophone with no trouble at all. Invented in 1842 by Adolphe Sax, the saxophone is a single-reed instrument like the clarinets. The bodies of these instruments have always been made of metal, and their shape and fingering mechanism are much the same today as they were in 1842.

After their invention, saxophones were quickly adopted in European military bands because of their strong sound, which blends well with both the other woodwinds and the brasses. Composers sometimes give the saxophone important solos with the orchestra because of its unique sound. In Modeste Moussorgsky's *Pictures at an Exhibition*, a haunting melody on the saxophone depicts the Old Castle. The saxophone's most important position, however, is in the fields of jazz and popular music. Although used sparingly in the orchestra, it has become a leading instrument in jazz, dance, concert, and marching bands.

Adolphe Sax built a complete family of saxophones with a total of fourteen different-sized instruments. Of the original fourteen sizes, three are in common use today: the E-flat alto, B-flat tenor, and E-flat baritone. Two others, the B-flat soprano and B-flat bass, are occasionally used to complete a saxophone choir. Since all saxophones are

SAXOPHONES

From left to right: Alto, Tenor, Baritone

played the same way and are similar to the clarinet, players often double on the clarinet and one of the saxophones.

The double-reed family of woodwinds consists of the

oboe, English horn, bassoon, and contrabassoon. Each has a double reed made of cane that the player holds between his lips and blows air through, just as you did earlier with the paper drinking straw.

There have been many types of double-reed instruments throughout history. Imported to Europe from the Orient, they have rather strange names such as bombarde, pommer, schryari, krummhorn, and rackett. It was during the seventeenth century that these instruments began taking on the appearance and sound of our modern instruments.

The oboe is the soprano of the double-reeds, and its nasal tone gives the tuning note for the other members of the orchestra. Its body is a hollow tube made of wood, and it is sometimes confused with the clarinet because of its similar appearance. However, the tone of the two instruments is very different, and they each have their own special parts to play.

OBOE

ENGLISH HORN

The English horn should really be called an alto oboe, since it is neither English nor technically a horn. It is simply a large oboe designed to play in the lower alto range. Its tone will remind you of a snake charmer, and it can be recognized easily because the bottom end of the wooden tube is shaped like a light bulb. The English horn alternates with the bass clarinet in playing the melody in the Arab Dance from Tchaikovsky's *Nutcracker Suite*—a most unusual combination of solo instruments.

The bassoon can play in either the tenor or the bass range. Its wooden body is nearly eight feet long but is folded in half to make it easier to hold. Although it has a fingering mechanism similar to the other woodwinds, the bassoon is the only wind instrument with more than two keys to be played with the thumbs. A bassoonist must

BASSOON

manage eight different keys with his left thumb and four with his right. Although a skilled bassoonist makes it look easy, he has practiced many hours in learning to manipulate all of those keys.

When played legato, the bassoon often plays the same part as the cello section. Its tone is similar to that of the cello and blends well with it. However, because of its ability to play wide leaps from high to low rapidly, the bassoon is often called upon to play comical-sounding melodies. It is nicknamed "the clown of the orchestra." When Paul Dukas composed "The Sorcerer's Apprentice," he wrote a funny little march to represent brooms-come-to-life fetching water from the river. The march is played, of course, by the bassoon.

The contrabassoon is the lowest-sounding instrument in the orchestra. Because its body is twice as long as the bassoon, nearly sixteen feet, it is folded into three sections. The sound of the vibrating double-reed travels down one part of the tube, makes a U turn and travels back up the middle section, makes another U turn to travel down the third section and out the bell. The sound that

CONTRABASSOON

comes out is so low that the floor seems to shake when it plays. Unlike the larger clarinets, the bassoon and contrabassoon are still made of wood.

The eighteen instruments of the four woodwind families, from the thirteen-inch piccolo to the sixteen-foot contrabassoon, have the widest range of sound from high to low and the greatest variety of tones of any group of instruments in the band or orchestra. Whether used as solo instruments, in various combinations, or all together, they provide the listener with a great variety of rich, vibrant sounds. It is no wonder that, with the exception of the voice, more boys and girls play woodwinds than any other group of instruments.

7

The Kitchen of the Orchestra

THE PERCUSSION FAMILY—DRUMS, MELODY, AND SOUND-EFFECT INSTRUMENTS

One of the most fascinating families of instruments is found in the very last row of the orchestra—the percussion section. Any instrument whose sound is made by striking, used only for special sound effects, and is not a member of one of the other instrument families is naturally assigned to the percussion section. Since it contains instruments of many different shapes, sizes, and sounds, it has been given the nickname "kitchen of the orchestra."

The drums are the most important group of instruments in the percussion family and the most powerful group of instruments in the band and orchestra. Their job is to emphasize the rhythms of the music with a variety of exciting sounds. At a symphony-orchestra concert, the roll of the tympani sounds like a mighty roll of thunder; watching a parade from the curb, our feet begin keeping time with the boom of the bass drum as the band marches past; and as we listen to popular music on the radio, we feel like dancing to the fancy rhythms played on the snare drum and tom-toms.

All boys and girls have played a drum at some time or another. It may not have been a real drum like those used in bands, but if you were beating a rhythm or keeping time with music by tapping on something, you were drumming.

When you were very young, you may have been given a pot and wooden spoon to play with. When you hit the bottom of the pot with the spoon, you were playing a simple drum. Another simple drum is an empty oatmeal box. By tapping out rhythms on the top of the round box with your fingers, the oatmeal box becomes an Indian drum, or tom-tom. It can even be painted bright colors, just like a real Indian tom-tom.

Nobody knows when the first drum was made, but the world's first drummer probably wore an animal skin for warmth, lived in a cave, and sent messages by hitting a hollow log with a stick. A hollow log doesn't have a very loud sound, just a dull *thunk;* however, primitive man found that he could send messages short distances by beating on the log in code. Since the code was in rhythm, he also discovered that it was fun to dance to the beat of the drum.

The first improvement to the hollow log drum was to stretch an animal skin tightly across one end of the log. By striking the skin rather than the log, primitive man improved the sound of his drum from a dull *thunk* to a resonant *BOOM*. Many tribes in Africa still send messages through the dark jungles by means of drum talk. They also use drums similar to the hollow-log drum to beat out rhythms for their tribal ceremonies and dances.

Modern drums used in bands and orchestras are musical instruments specially made for their job of emphasizing rhythms. The log has been replaced by a round, hollow shell made of wood, metal, or plastic, and instead of an animal skin, a thin sheet of plastic called a head is stretched across the open ends of the shell. The drums are played by striking the heads with wooden sticks, fingers, or beaters whose ends are covered with a soft material like felt or lamb's wool.

Although there are many different drums, the ones you see most often are the snare drum, bass drum, and tympani (kettledrums). The snare drum is the smallest and has the highest sound. Its shell is four to ten inches deep and about fifteen inches across the opening. A set of wires stretched across the bottom head, called snares, gives this drum its name. Also, the snares vibrate against the head when the drum is struck and create its characteristic sound. Played by striking the top head with a pair of wooden sticks, the snare drum tone is a crisp *rrrat-a-tat-tat, rrrat-a-tat-tat*.

As mentioned earlier, the snare drum has been an important military instrument, along with the bugle and fife, for hundreds of years. For example, it has been used by armies all over the world to signal soldiers to advance or retreat (hence the phrase "beat a retreat"), listen for an important announcement, and march in step. Even today, a loud drum roll is used to get the attention of a crowd, and marching bands often have an entire row of snare drummers playing fancy rhythms to help marchers keep in step.

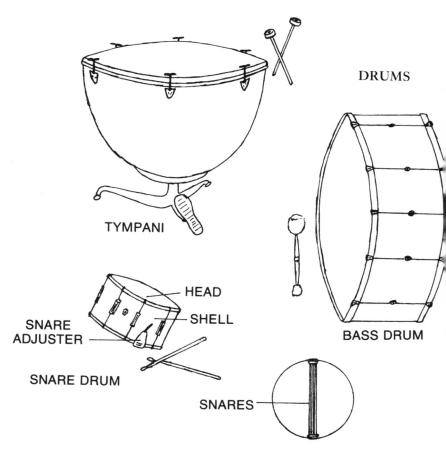

DRUMS

TYMPANI

BASS DRUM

HEAD

SHELL

SNARE ADJUSTER

SNARE DRUM

SNARES

The bass drum is much larger than the snare drum, and its sound is a big *BOOM*. The head of the drum is struck with a beater that has a soft ball on the end. The shell measures several feet across the opening. Bass drums used in marching bands are often so big that they can't be carried. Instead, they are pulled on a cart while the player walks alongside it beating out the rhythm.

The tympani are different because they can be tuned to a definite pitch. The tympani shell looks like a very large bowl, or kettle, made of copper. The head is stretched across the top of the bowl. The player is able to tune the tympani by pushing on foot pedals attached to a tuning mechanism inside the drum. Since each tympani can only be tuned to four or five different pitches, they are used in sets. As many as five drums of various sizes are played by one drummer (tympanist), whose job is to tune each tympani to the proper pitch and play the correct rhythms, volumes, and sometimes melodies.

In addition to the drums, there is a large group of instruments that add a special sound to the rhythms, including the cymbals, triangle, tambourine, wood block, maracas, claves, and many more. These instruments have been gathered from all over the world, and many of them give the listener a hint about the origin of the music being played. The cymbals, and their cousin, the gong, are important in Oriental music. Castanets give the music a Spanish flavor. Music from Latin American countries usually includes the maracas and claves, as well as many different-sized drums.

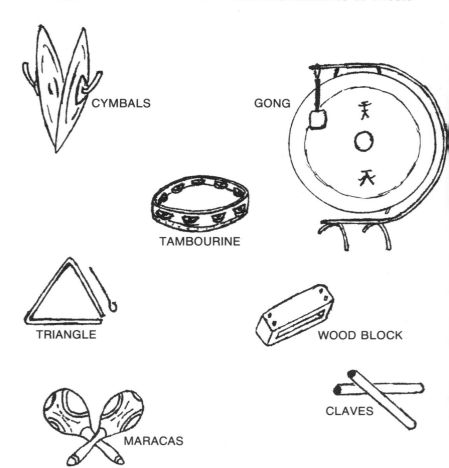

CYMBALS

GONG

TAMBOURINE

TRIANGLE

WOOD BLOCK

MARACAS

CLAVES

CASTANETS

SPECIAL RHYTHM INSTRUMENTS

Musicians have also learned to use this special group of instruments in new and different ways. As an example, the cymbals have many uses. When two cymbals are crashed together, they provide important accents to the music; complicated rhythms are played by striking one cymbal with a drum stick, which is an important part of jazz music; and when the player uses a pair of sticks to roll on a cymbal, the sound is very shimmery and mysterious.

There is a smaller group of instruments whose job is to play melodies. They have a series of wooden or metal bars tuned to definite pitches that are arranged in a chromatic row just like the keys of a piano. The bars are struck with either plastic or metal mallets. The smaller instruments in this group, orchestra bells (glockenspiel) and bell lyra, have a high-pitched tone like the ping of small bells. The chimes, which have long metal tubes rather than bars, have a sound like the bong of a large clock. Other instruments in this group are the xylophone, marimba, and vibraharp (vibes).

The sound-effects instruments of the percussion family add even more variety to the music. There are coconut-shells to represent the clip-clop of horses' hooves, bird whistles, and instruments that sound like the roar of a lion and the bark of a dog. The exciting music from *West Side Story* by Leonard Bernstein uses sirens and police whistles, and Tchaikovsky's "1812 Overture" even calls for the firing of several cannon.

One of the most important instruments in the percussion family is not one, but a combination of

MARIMBA

XYLOPHONE

Dave Chare Photography

Courtesy J. C. Deagan, Inc.

VIBRAHARP
Courtesy J. C. Deagan, Inc.

ORCHESTRA CHIMES
Courtesy J. C. Deagan, Inc.

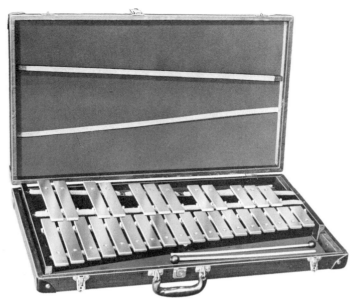

GLOCKENSPIEL
Courtesy J. C. Deagan, Inc.

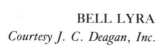
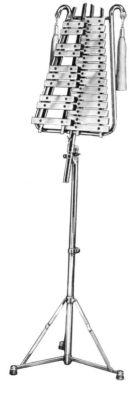

BELL LYRA
Courtesy J. C. Deagan, Inc.

instruments—the drum set. In the early 1900's, when dixieland and jazz music were just beginning, an unknown drummer fastened a foot pedal to a bass drum so that he could play rhythms on the snare drum with his hands and keep the beat with the bass drum at the same time. Over the years, drummers have added other instruments to this bass-snare drum combination until it has become a one-man percussion section.

The drum set is most often used in small groups and in the fields of popular and jazz music. It usually consists of a bass drum, snare drum, tom-tom, hi-hat (two small cymbals crashed together by means of a second foot pedal), and one or more cymbals of different sizes. These are all gathered closely around the player within easy reach of his hands and feet. Most players specialize their set by adding other drums and attaching wood blocks, cow bells, and other smaller instruments to the bass drum.

The sounds of the drum set are exciting, and a skilled player makes it look easy to play. Without many years of practice, however, playing a drum set would be like patting your head with one hand, rubbing your stomach with the other, and walking up the stairs backward, all at the same time.

Unlike musicians in the other sections of the orchestra who usually specialize in one or perhaps two instruments, members of the percussion section must be able to play all of the percussion instruments. A drummer plays the drums, period. But a musician who can play all of the

DRUM SET

instruments in the "kitchen" is a percussionist. Boys and girls learning to play the snare drum in school can look forward to the day when they can play all of the percussion instruments well enough to deserve that title.

8

The Harp and Keyboard Instruments

HARP, PIANO, AND PIPE ORGAN

The earliest musical instruments could be played only one note at a time. By playing a series of notes, one after another, the musician created melodies. For thousands of years, men were content with playing simple melodies occasionally accented with the beat of a drum or cymbal.

During the Middle Ages (sixth to fifteenth centuries) musicians and composers began using instruments in combination to express their musical ideas. They found that two or more melodies, if written just right, could be played at the same time and sound both interesting and pleasing. This type of music is called polyphony. Singing "Row, Row, Row Your Boat" as a round is an example of polyphonic music. They also found that certain notes could be played at the same time to form chords. By experimenting with these chords, they then learned how they could be used to accompany melodies. This kind of music is called homophony, although a more familiar word for music using chords is harmony.

In order to play polyphonic and homophonic music, it was necessary for groups of musicians to gather together and to form choirs, orchestras, and bands. Some of the musicians would play or sing the melody, others would play chords forming the harmony, or, if it was polyphonic music, they would divide up to play the contrasting melodies.

As people learned to understand and appreciate the new sounds of polyphony and harmony, a group of instruments began to develop that would allow one musician to play all of the parts with no help from others. Instead of several musicians playing single-note instruments only one musician with one instrument was needed. The most important members of this group are the harp, piano, and organ. Of course, these instruments didn't replace single-note instruments, but they are often used to accompany them. Today they are played as solo instruments and in combination with other instruments.

The harp is one of man's oldest musical instruments. The simple idea of making a musical sound with a vibrating string probably came from early man's hearing the twang of the bowstring as a hunter shot an arrow. The earliest record of this idea being used on harplike instruments especially made to play music is found in Babylonian inscriptions of over four thousand years ago.

Early harps were small enough to carry easily. They were either U-shaped, similar to a hunter's bow, or V-shaped. One or more strings of different lengths were stretched from one side to the other. The melodies and harmonies played on these harps were limited to a few notes, depending upon the number of strings that could be stretched tightly between the sides of the frame without its breaking.

The sounds of the small harp have always delighted man. In many parts of the world, it has been a favorite instrument to accompany singing and dancing for thousands of years. In ancient Britain and Ireland, especially, small harps were favorites of the bards, singing poets who traveled from town to town. In fact, the people of Ireland loved the harp so much that they made it their national emblem, and it still appears on Ireland's coat-of-arms.

The student harp, first introduced in 1961, has no pedals and only 33 strings. The strings are tuned to the C-Major scale, but individual strings can be raised one half step by flipping a small lever at the top end of the string.

The modern harp is much too large to be carried so easily, and a station wagon or truck is necessary to transport it. Despite its size, however, the harp has an elegant shape and delicate tone. Its beautiful sound will make you think of angels. Since its sound is as light and graceful as the movement of dancers, the harp has become a favorite instrument of ballet-music composers. Tchaikovsky often

STUDENT HARP (LEFT) AND CONCERT HARP

used it in his music, as in the lovely cadenza introducing the Waltz of the Flowers in his *Nutcracker Suite*.

The body of the harp is shaped much like a triangle, consisting of a hollow pillar that sits on a base in front of the player, a slanting sound box, which rests back on the player's shoulder, and a gracefully curved neck across the top. There are forty-seven strings stretched from the sound box to the neck. Each string is tuned to one of the seven notes of the major scale, and the player must check the tuning of each of the strings before every concert or practice session.

The harp is played by plucking the strings with the thumb and first three fingers of each hand. The most beautiful and special sound of the harp is the glissando. To play this, the harpist strums the strings in a broad sweeping motion of his hands. The harp has one of the widest ranges of any instrument in the orchestra, and the sounds of the glissando can go from very high to very low.

The strings are all made from either wire or catgut and, except for their length and thickness, look very similar. The mystery of how the player knows which strings to play is a good one, but the secret is that some of the strings are colored. All of the C strings are red, and all of the F strings are blue. With the help of these guide strings, the player can quickly and easily see if his hands are in the right place.

In order for the harp to play the chromatic notes in the scale, it has a pedal mechanism that allows the harpist to change the pitch of the strings as he plays. There are seven

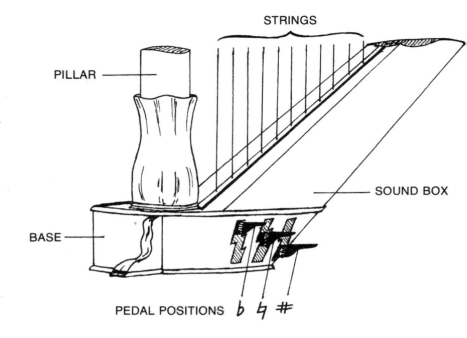

PILLAR

STRINGS

SOUND BOX

BASE

PEDAL POSITIONS ♭ ♮ ♯

HARP PEDALS

pedals attached to the base of the harp (four on one side, and three on the other), one of each note of the major scale, and each pedal has three positions. In the top position the strings are tuned to the notes of the C-flat major scale. When the player pushes one of the pedals with his feet, it raises all of the strings of a certain pitch either one or two half steps. For example, when the C-string pedal is pushed down one notch, all of the C strings are raised from C-flat to C-natural. Pushing the pedal down to the next notch raises the strings from C-natural to C-sharp.

Operating seven pedals makes the harp more difficult to play, but the invention of this mechanism in 1810 was a very important step in the development of the modern harp. Since that time, composers have written much beautiful music for the harp, and in addition to its jobs as soloist and accompanist for other instruments, it has gained an important position in the string section of the orchestra.

Other instruments in this group have complicated sound mechanisms that are operated by pushing a lever, or key. If you were to look inside a piano or organ, you would see several hundred different parts, but despite this complex mechanism, all the player has to do is press the right key to make music.

The keyboard, as we know it, was first developed over eight hundred years ago. It is a series of white and black keys arranged side by side within reach of the player's hands. The white keys are the notes of the C major scale. The smaller black keys are the chromatic notes not in that scale, the sharps and flats. If you look closely, you will see that the black keys are in groups of twos and threes. To find the key for C, locate the white key just to the left of any group of two black keys. If you press down a C key on the right end of the keyboard, the note will be very high, and on the left end the C will be very low.

What happens when you press one of the keys in different in each instrument. The harpsichord, cousin of the piano, has many strings under its lid. When one the keys is pressed down, a small pin or quill is caused to pluck one of the strings. The sound is somewhat like a harp and very

The harpsichord is played by a tiny quill plucking the string when the key is pressed. After plucking the string, the quill falls away from the string, allowing it to vibrate freely. When the key is released, the quill returns to its starting point, and the damper stops the string's vibrations.

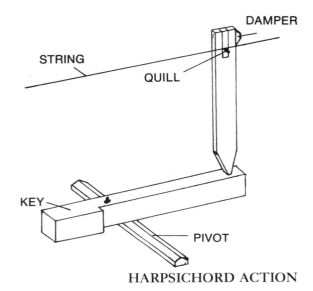

HARPSICHORD ACTION

CLAVICHORD ACTION

The sound-producing mechanism of a keyboard instrument is called the action. In the clavichord action, a metal tangent strikes the string. It raises the string slightly and stays in contact with it until the key is released. As the tangent falls away, the string returns to its original position, and the cloth damper stops its vibrations.

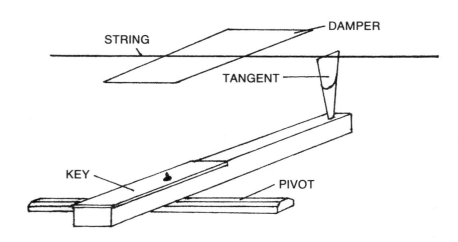

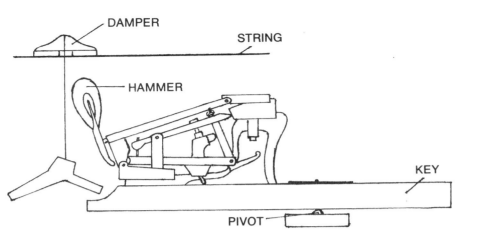

DAMPER

STRING

HAMMER

KEY

PIVOT

PIANO ACTION

When a piano key is pressed, the hammer is caused to fly up and strike the string forcefully and immediately fall away so that the string's vibrations aren't deadened. At the same instant, the damper is lifted from the string. The damper drops back onto the string to stop its vibrations, and the hammer returns to its original position when the key is released.

soft. A similar instrument is the clavichord. The most important difference between the two is that when a key is pressed down on the calvichord a small hammer (tangent) strikes one of the strings. The sound is still very soft, but the player can play a little louder or softer by striking the key harder or more gently.

The idea of using a hammer mechanism to start the strings vibrating was used in the first piano. With the invention of a new mechanism to operate the hammers in 1709, instrument makers developed a keyboard instrument capable of playing a wide range of dynamics, from crashing chords to a feathery wisp of sound. Being the first stringed keyboard instrument capable of playing both very soft and very loud, it became known as a *piano e forte*, which means "soft and loud" in Italian.

The piano is certainly one of the most popular musical instruments. It took nearly a hundred years after its invention to replace the then popular harpsichord and clavichord, but when it was finally accepted, it became important as a solo instrument, a tool for both composers and conductors, and a basic instrument for training music students. It has been estimated that today over 22 million people in the United States play the piano, from very young children to professional musicians.

Its eighty-eight keys give the piano the widest range of any instrument except the pipe organ. It is capable of producing thundering chords in the very low range and light, bell-like sounds in the very high range. Skilled players can make the beautiful music written by the composers such as Beethoven and Chopin sing through a large concert hall. Others have found the piano equally good at playing the many styles of jazz and popular music.

Composers and conductors use the piano to try out music that is intended for large groups. The composer will first write a symphony as piano music. When the symphony is completed, he will rewrite the music for the many instruments of the orchestra that will play the different parts. Similarly, the conductor of an orchestra will often play the music on the piano before the musicians gather for a rehearsal. In this way he can learn what all of

GRAND PIANO (STEINWAY)

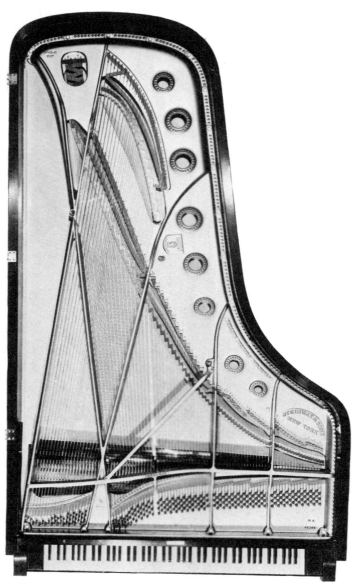

GRAND PIANO (TOP VIEW SHOWING INSIDES)

UPRIGHT PIANO

the parts are supposed to sound like and be prepared to help the musicians fit their many parts together.

The piano is probably the most important instrument for training students in music. Whether or not a student wants to become a composer, conductor, or professional pianist, learning to play the piano certainly makes a person a better listener. It has also been found that a boy or girl who has studied melody, harmony, and musical style while learning to play piano learns to play other instruments better and more quickly.

When a key is pressed down on a pipe organ, a stream of air is directed through a series of pipes to produce the tone. The organ's earliest ancestor is probably the same as

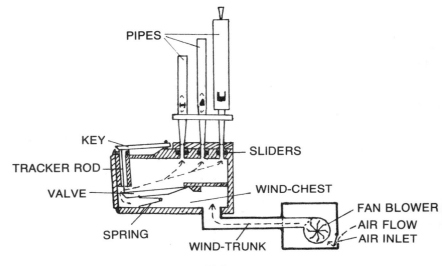

PIPES

KEY

TRACKER ROD

VALVE

SPRING

SLIDERS

WIND-CHEST

FAN BLOWER
AIR FLOW
AIR INLET

WIND-TRUNK

PIPE ORGAN MECHANISM

Since the pipe organ is a wind instrument, its entire mechanism deals with the supply and control of air. In this diagram, the air supply is provided by an electric fan blower, housed in a sound-proof box. The blower draws air in through the air inlet and blows it through the wind-trunk, filling the wind-chest with a ready supply of air.

The air flow is controlled by the organ's action, consisting of the key, tracker rod, and valve. The valve is held closed by a spring and the lightly compressed air inside of the wind-chest. When the key is pressed, its downward movement is transferred to the valve by the tracker rod, and the valve opens. This allows the air to flow to the pipes and produce the organ's sound. Each key may control the air flow to several pipes, each having the same pitch but a different tone; one pipe might sound like a flute, another more like an oboe, while both play the same note.

The final control of the air is by the sliders. These determine which pipes the air can go through. The organist operates them by means of stops (not shown). The stops cause the sliders either to open or close the holes leading to certain pipes, altering the organ's tone quality.

that of the woodwind instruments—the pipes of Pan. However, the pipes of a large organ are much bigger than Pan's. They range in size from a few inches to several feet in length, are often stored in a special pipe room near the organ, and are operated by a complicated mechanism.

In early organs, the air was provided by bellows, which were pumped by young boys. If the bellows weren't pumped hard enough, the clumsy mechanism would operate only with great difficulty. When this happened, the player had the choice of either using his fist to push down the keys or spanking the boy so he would pump harder.

The key mechanism and method of providing the air stream have been changed and improved over the years. There are even electronic organs that attempt to imitate the sound of pipe organs with tones created by an electrical current. These electronic organs often come very close in their imitation, but the strong, majestic tone of a large pipe organ is still very impressive to hear. Once regarded as the king of instruments, the pipe organ is capable of playing from very soft to nearly as loud as a full symphony orchestra while producing a wide variety of different tone colors.

The golden age of organ making and playing was the seventeenth and eighteenth centuries. During those years great organs were constructed in churches and cathedrals throughout Europe. Musicians like Johann Sebastian Bach would travel many miles just for a chance to play on one of those magnificent instruments. Many organs from that period are still in use, and newer instruments are often patterned after them.

PIPE ORGAN

Most pipe organs have at least three keyboards. Two or more are played with the hands and are called manuals. One is played with the feet and is called a pedalboard. In addition to the pedalboard and several manuals, the player must also operate a series of tabs or knobs, called stops.

Adjusting the stops directs the air to different combinations of pipes and alters the tone quality of the organ. Besides being able to imitate the tone quality of many other wind instruments, the pipe organ has its own unique tone that no other instrument can imitate.

An organ is difficult to play and an organ teacher will usually not take a student unless he can already play the piano quite well. There are three steps in becoming an organist, and the first is to become a skilled pianist. Second, you must find an organ teacher who will accept you as a student. Finally, you must be near a church, cathedral, or other large building that houses an organ so that you will have an instrument to play. If you follow these three steps and practice hard, someday you might be fortunate enough to play on one of the great organs of Europe that Bach played many years ago.

9
Creating Musical Sounds with Electricity

ELECTRONIC INSTRUMENTS—
TAPE RECORDER, SYNTHESIZER,
COMPUTER

Electricity has become very important in today's
music. We can listen to our favorite music
whenever we want because it has been recorded on
phonograph records and tapes; we can hear music being
played in another city by turning a switch on the radio or
television set; instruments with soft sounds can be heard
even in large auditoriums by the use of amplifiers and
loudspeakers; and modern composers are able to write
music in new styles using the sounds created by the tape
recorder, synthesizer, and computer—twentieth-century
instruments of music.

Throughout history, man has searched for new musical
sounds and improved ways of producing them. Early man
had an idea that the sound of a vibrating string could be

used to make music. He built simple instruments using that idea, which have led to our present violin, harp, and guitar. As he learned to make things with metal, he also used it to make musical instruments. Over the last five hundred years, many instruments have been improved by adding valve, key, and pedal mechanisms. In the same way, twentieth-century man has continued the search for new sounds by using the idea of producing sounds with an electrical current.

The scientific study of electricity didn't begin until the late 1500's. Since that time, many men have helped us learn to use electricity in many different ways. One of those men was Ben Franklin, who, in 1752, flew a kite during a thunderstorm to study the electricity in clouds.

Another was Thomas Edison, who invented the first machine to become important in music—the phonograph. Although Edison's machine was operated by hand, an improved version that used an electric motor was exhibited the following year. Later improvements led to recordings being made using electric microphones and amplifiers and played on all-electric phonographs.

Edison invented the phonograph in 1877, and by the turn of the century the radio and magnetic wire recorder (ancestor of the tape recorder) had been invented and were in use. In 1906 the first electric musical instrument was demonstrated in Holyoke, Massachusetts—the Dynamophone. The instrument was played by a keyboard, used telephone wires to send its music, and weighed over two

hundred tons. Even though the Dynamophone was exper-
imental, it quickly led to the invention of many different
types of electrical instruments.

Perhaps the best known of the very early electronic
instruments was the Theremin. Introduced in the early
1920's, the Theremin's sounds were controlled by waving
one hand over a horizontal volume antenna and the other
along a vertical pitch antenna. The result was an electronic signal that sounded like a strange, eerie whistle,
perfect for the background sounds in a space-adventure
movie.

THEREMIN

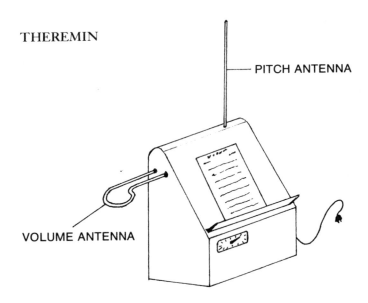

PITCH ANTENNA

VOLUME ANTENNA

The electric organ was invented by Laurens Hammond of Chicago in 1934. Instead of being an entirely new instrument, the Hammond organ was intended as a less expensive substitute for the pipe organ. By using electronic components instead of the usual pipes, the Hammond organ could be built both much cheaper and much smaller. Many of the ideas used by Hammond in developing his instrument helped other builders of electronic instruments in their search for new devices that would produce new sounds.

Most of the early electronic instruments are now either forgotten or in museums. Except for the electric organ, none has any importance in music any longer. However, as each new instrument came along, it would excite composers who were searching for new sounds to express their musical ideas. They would carefully explore its possibilities for use in modern music and write music using its sounds.

During the 1930's, many composers began experimenting with phonograph records and a technique called sound distortion. They found that new sounds could be created if a record was played backward, had scratches made in the grooves, or was played at a different speed. For example, if a recording of a trumpet was played backward and at a faster or slower speed, a new, nontrumpet sound was created. John Cage was an important composer of this kind of music. He even wrote music that called for an ensemble of several radios and phonographs to be played at the same time.

Nearly any boy or girl can experiment with sounds in much the same way as did the composers of the 1930's. First, try playing a record on the phonograph either at a different speed (a 45 rpm record at 78 rpm's) or touching the edge of the record slightly to get different speeds. If it is a stereo record, try turning off one of the speakers to cut out part of the music. Next, add the sounds coming from a radio. Experiment by turning the volume of the radio just high enough so that its sounds blend with those from the stereo, turning the volume up and down in rhythm, turning the radio to a news broadcast rather than a music station, or tune it so that there is more static than music.

Blend the sounds, mix them, change them any way you like, or add another radio; there are no rules to follow. Whether or not the sounds you "compose" could be called music is up to you, but best of all, you will find that it is fun to experiment with sounds produced by the use of electricity.

This type of experimenting and composing was continued during the 1940's and was developed into tape music. Magnetic recording tape, first used on a large scale about 1950, was much easier to work with than disc records. Recorded sounds were easier to alter and edit, making the creation of new sounds even easier for composers of modern music. Composers like John Cage began writing music for ensembles of tape recorders to be played both alone and along with traditional instruments. Such music is called *musique concrete*.

Even though the tape recorder is not an instrument that

you would take lessons on and hope to play in a band, in some ways it is similar to the trumpet. The trumpet takes the sound of the player's vibrating lip and changes the soft buzz into the brilliant sound we are used to hearing. This brilliant sound can be altered by placing a mute in the bell of the trumpet, and the pitch can be changed by pressing valves in various combinations.

The tape recorder, on the other hand, can take any sound and change it. The sound of water running from a faucet can be recorded on tape, played at a different speed, played backward, or edited in many different ways. This familiar sound then becomes a new sound, a sound so unique that it could never have been heard before the invention of recording equipment—just as the brilliant sound of a modern trumpet could never have been heard before the discovery and use of metal.

Perhaps the most important electronic instrument of the twentieth century is the synthesizer. In 1955, RCA introduced the Olson-Belar Sound Synthesizer, a large electronic device capable of producing entirely new sounds, instead of altering sounds, as does the tape recorder. Although smaller than the two hundred-ton Dynamophone, this new machine takes up one entire wall of the room where it is kept at Columbia University in New York.

The synthesizer's introduction caused much excitement among composers interested in electronic music. However, the RCA machine was very expensive to build, complicated to operate, and very large. The next important step was for a smaller instrument to be developed. Only in this way would composers be able to write music using a synthesizer without having to travel to Columbia University.

Several different styles of smaller synthesizers were introduced during the 1960's. Even though each of the new instruments was designed after the RCA giant, their smaller size kept them from doing as much as the RCA machine. However, composers all over the country and throughout the world were delighted with the smaller instruments and immediately went to work composing music for them. Today, synthesizers of various sizes and styles are found in recording studios and in college music departments everywhere. Many rock bands and popular music groups even use a small synthesizer along with guitars, drums, and other instruments.

The synthesizer is the most complicated instrument of music ever invented. It consists of several modules (small boxes about the size of a transistor radio) that are housed in a cabinet along with an internal power supply and all of the plugs, wires, and other electrical equipment necessary for it to function. Depending upon the style of the machine, it is operated by either a pianolike keyboard, a series of touch plates, or a key-punch board. Composers working with the synthesizer find that it is very helpful to have a background in electrical engineering as well as music.

There is no way to describe the sounds produced by a synthesizer, because they can produce nearly any sound a

PORTABLE SYNTHESIZER

composer can imagine. You can buy recordings of synthesizer music, but you hear their sounds every day and don't know it. Much of the background music for movies and television includes the sounds of a synthesizer; many radio networks use synthesizer music as the lead-in to news broadcasts; and the Broadway show *Jesus Christ, Super Star* included synthesizers in the orchestra.

If you are listening to some music and can't identify the instrument playing it, you could be hearing a synthesizer. However, traditional music played on a synthesizer might fool you. Not long ago, a record entitled *Switched-On Bach* became a best seller. Although the music consisted of compositions by the great Baroque composer J. S. Bach, they were performed entirely on a synthesizer.

About the same time the RCA synthesizer was introduced, men began experimenting with the computer as an instrument of music. High-speed computers are used for many things, and it seemed only natural that they might also have a musical use. The computer doesn't produce any of its own musical sounds, but three different musical uses have been developed.

One use is to combine the computer with a synthesizer. In this combination, the computer controls the settings on the synthesizer modules and creates a supersynthesizer. Another use of the computer is to compose music. Used in this way, the composer programs all of the necessary information into the computer, which then fits the information together into a composition to be performed by other instruments. A third use is in performance. Although the computer makes no sound itself, it can be programmed to produce information, which is then processed as musical sounds on magnetic tape and played through amplifiers and loud speakers.

Much serious electronic music is being composed and performed. One of the most important compositions for tape recorder is *Poème Electronique* by Edgar Varese. Known as the Father of Electronic Music, Varese composed this piece to be performed continuously at the 1958 World's Fair in Brussels. Other compositions, combining the sounds of traditional musical instruments and tape recorders or synthesizers, are being included in orchestra concert programs.

Two pioneers in electronic music, Vladimir Ussachevsky and Karlheinz Stockhausen, provide excellent examples of *musique concrete*. In his "Transposition," Ussachevsky tape-records a single tone, the lowest note of the piano, and creates an entire musical composition by altering it in many different ways. In Stockhausen's "Gesang der Jüglinge" ("Youths' Song"), he records the sounds of children's voices, uses *musique concrete* techniques to manipulate the sounds, and then adds them to the pure electronic sound of the synthesizer.

Many recordings of electronic music can be found in the record collection of your library. For your first listening experience, select a short composition, read the information about it on the record jacket, and listen to it at least twice. Some of the music will sound very strange to your ears, especially if you expect to hear familiar sounds. However, if you listen expecting to hear something new and unfamiliar, you will discover many very exciting sounds.

Nobody knows whether computers, synthesizers, and tape recorders will still be used to make music in the year 1999. Early man started with the idea of using a vibrating string to make music. Since that time, many string instruments have been invented. Some of these instruments have disappeared, some have been improved beyond recognition, and others have been replaced by even newer instruments. But the idea of using the sound of a vibrating string remains an important part of music.

In the same way, many different electronic instruments have already been invented. The Dynamophone has disappeared from use, the synthesizer has gone through many changes and improvements in its short life, and the disc phonograph record has been joined by magnetic recording tape. The instruments will continue to change, but the idea of using electricity to make music will certainly continue to be important for many years.

Index